KOFI ANNAN

The Peacekeeper
by John Tessitore

A Book Report Biography
FRANKLIN WATTS
A Division of Grolier Publishing
New York / London / Hong Kong / Sydney
Danbury, Connecticut

For United Nations workers around the world,
because they still believe in peace

Frontispiece: Secretary-General Kofi Annan at Macalester College commencement on May 17, 1998

Cover illustration by Gary Overacre, interpreted from a photograph by © Corbis-Bettmann/Henny Ray Abrams.

Photographs ©: AP/Wide World Photos: 76 (Patrick Aviolat), 83 (Shawn Baldwin), 71 (Richard Drew), 59 (Marty Lederhandler), 65 (Santiago Lyon), 79 (UN Photo by Evan Schneider), 13; Archive Photos: 22, 40; Corbis Sygma: 8 (Allan Tannenbaum), 37; Corbis-Bettmann: 42 (Hulton Deutsch Collection), 53 (Jon Simon), 34 (UPI), 19, 23, 25; Liaison Agency, Inc.: 51 (Alain Morvan), 61 (Scott Daniel Peterson); Macalester College: 30, 31, 33; Martin A. Levick: 45, 74; Steve Woit: 2; United Nations/DPI: 11, 26, 48, 15 (John Isaac).

Visit Franklin Watts on the Internet at:
http://publishing.grolier.com

Library of Congress Cataloging-in-Publication Data

Tessitore, John.
    Kofi Annan : the peacekeeper / by John Tessitore.
        p. cm. — (Book report biography)
    Includes bibliography references and index.
    Summary : A biography of the Ghanaian statesman who was elected Secretary General of the United Nations in 1997.
    ISBN 0-531-11706-5
    1. Annan, Kofi A. (Kofi Atta)—Juvenile literature. 2. World politics—1998—Juvenile literature. 3. United Nations—Biography—Juvenile literature. 4. Statesmen—Ghana—Biography—Juvenile literature. [1. Annan, Kofi A. (Kofi Atta). 2. Statesmen. 3. United Nations—Biography.] I. Title. II. Series.

    D839.7.A56 A3 2000
    341.23'092—dc21
    [B]   99-462180

CONTENTS

THE WORLD STAGE

In the early months of 1998, relations between the United States and the Middle Eastern nation of Iraq were deteriorating. They threatened to touch off yet another war in the Middle East—a conflict involving many countries from around the world. Kofi Annan was the last hope for peace.

A year earlier, Annan had taken over as the seventh secretary-general of the United Nations (UN), making him the most important figure in an organization dedicated to international peace and the betterment of humanity. As secretary-general, Annan also became the first modern international leader to have been born and raised in black Africa. To people of African descent in every nation—people who were often denied important government offices because of discrimination—Annan's election was a source of hope.

Kofi Annan is congratulated after his appointment as the seventh UN secretary-general.

As a result, Annan was already a hero in early 1998, but he was still new to his job. He had to assure world leaders that they had chosen wisely when they elected him. He had to prove that he could be a strong leader in a time of crisis. Most world leaders already admired Annan for his even temper and his ability to end disputes when he had held smaller jobs at the United Nations.

Annan's first important mission as the world's leading diplomat was a most difficult task. For decades, the Middle East has been a region of intense religious and political conflict. For a man on a mission of peace, a man trying to prove himself to the international community, there are few more complicated regions in the world.

MOUNTING TENSIONS WITH HUSSEIN

Negotiations with Saddam Hussein, the president of Iraq, had never been easy. In 1990, Hussein had directed Iraqi troops to invade the neighboring nation of Kuwait, a small country rich in oil. A group of countries, including the United States, the United Kingdom, and Canada, united in the Persian Gulf War to remove Iraqi troops from Kuwait and keep Hussein from taking over other oil-producing Middle Eastern nations. The United Nations passed a resolution that all member nations should stop trading with Iraq.

After the war ended and Iraq withdrew from Kuwait, the allies signed agreements at the United Nations. In the cease-fire agreement, Iraq agreed to destroy all its biological and chemical weapons and any facilities for manufacturing nuclear weapons. The war had devastated Iraq, and people faced terrible hardships, including limited supplies of food and medicine.

The allies were willing to trade again with Iraq under one condition—Saddam Hussein had to prove that he was no longer hiding and maintaining his most dangerous weapons. Known as "weapons of mass destruction," they included nuclear missiles and chemical and biological weapons—poisons that can kill thousands of people when released in the air. Hussein said many times that he did not have such weapons. But officials from the United Nations who were sent to inspect Iraqi military warehouses reported that Hussein would not cooperate with them and suspected that he was hiding weapons in secret places.

Tensions over the UN inspections eventually drove the United States and Iraq into a direct confrontation. In 1997, U.S. aircraft carriers moved into the Persian Gulf, ready to attack Iraq, while Hussein rallied his own armies to defend his nation. Only Kofi Annan was willing to negotiate with Hussein at this point, and only a successful negotiation would preserve peace in the region. Few people were confident that Annan could prevent a war.

A camera crew from the popular American television show *60 Minutes* flew with Annan to Baghdad, the capital city of Iraq, in February 1998. The crew members were amazed that, as the world watched nervously and feared another war, Annan seemed relaxed and confident, calm enough to take a short nap. But when the plane touched ground outside of Baghdad, Annan was ready to negotiate. He immediately met with Iraq's deputy prime minister, Tariq Aziz, who was wearing a military uniform to show Annan that Iraq was prepared to fight.

The next day, Annan and Aziz negotiated for an hour and twenty minutes, almost a full hour longer than scheduled. During that time, they

In February 1998, Kofi Annan flew to Iraq to negotiate with Iraq's deputy prime minister, Tariq Aziz (at right in military uniform).

thoughtfully discussed plans for an agreement that Annan brought with him from the United Nations. The negotiations were going surprisingly smoothly. Then Annan heard that he was to meet face-to-face with Saddam Hussein. Such a meeting was unexpected, but Annan welcomed the opportunity.

MEETING WITH HUSSEIN

On February 22, 1998, three black cars pulled into the driveway of the huge mansion in Baghdad where Annan was staying. Annan, three advisors, and a bodyguard got into the cars and went to Hussein's nearby Republican Presidential Palace.

When they arrived at the palace, Annan suggested that he and Hussein leave their advisors and talk privately about the possibility of a peaceful agreement. As one of his advisors said later, the private meeting was a wise choice for Annan: "If you told Saddam Hussein in front of other people, 'Unless you do this, a strike is inevitable,' he's the kind of man who would say, 'I can't give in to threats. So be it, and goodbye.' But in private, you can tell him about it." The men were together for three hours, smoking cigars and discussing their options as the United States and its allies

Annan and Saddam Hussein negotiating at the Iraqi leader's palace in Baghdad

surrounded Iraq with soldiers, ships, and planes ready to attack.

Finally, the two men reached an agreement. Hussein assured Annan that he was not afraid of the United States—he was ready to fight another war. But he agreed to cooperate with the United Nations because he admired and respected Annan.

Annan understood that Hussein did not like

to be bullied. As he said later, "The sense of humiliation or losing your dignity or losing face—[the Iraqis] would die or go to war over that." So without threatening or scolding Hussein, Annan convinced him to allow UN inspectors to search the eight hiding places most likely to hold weapons of mass destruction. In return, the United Nations would ease the harsh trading regulations. With that agreement, the threat of war receded. Annan had succeeded in his first important global assignment as secretary-general.

PRESIDENTIAL PRAISE

President Bill Clinton announced shortly after the agreement that Kofi Annan "deserves thanks" from the people of the United States and the rest of the world for preserving peace. Even one of Annan's harshest critics, U.S. senator Jesse Helms, had to express his admiration for the secretary-general. "Given what you had to work with," Helms told Annan, "you did a very good job."

As the world praised him, however, the famously calm, even-tempered secretary-general refused to accept all the credit. On the flight back to New York from Baghdad, Annan broke out a bottle of champagne and toasted his advisors and coworkers for all their hard work. "He's disarmingly modest," said Mike Wallace, the *60 Minutes*

During his time in Iraq, Kofi Annan was interviewed by Mike Wallace from the television show 60 Minutes.

reporter who covered the negotiations with Hussein. In this case, as in many others in his long career with the United Nations, Kofi Annan's modesty was a great asset.

The tension between Iraq and the United States did not end in February 1998. Two months after Annan and Hussein signed the agreement, UN weapons inspectors reported that Hussein was still not cooperating with their search for weapons of mass destruction. As a result, many of the regulations against trade with Iraq were still in place. But Annan had preserved the peace in his February meetings with Hussein and proved that he was a capable leader in complicated times. Perhaps more importantly, he proved to the world that the United Nations could be a powerful, successful mediator in international disputes.

This is the story of Kofi Annan, the man responsible for world peace in the beginning of the twenty-first century.

CHAPTER ONE

CHILD OF FREEDOM

Kofi Atta Annan was born on April 8, 1938, in Kumasi, an inland city in the British colony then known as the Gold Coast (now Ghana). Kofi's ancestors on both his mother's and father's side were chiefs of the Fante people.

The Fante ethnic group inhabits a small section of West Africa. Originally, they lived along the western Atlantic coast, but they began to move inland more than 300 years ago. They came into contact with Europeans who were exploring and colonizing Africa, creating their own settlements and imposing their own governments on the African people.

KOFI'S FAMILY

The Fante learned to work with the Europeans, however. By the time Kofi was born, many Fante held important jobs in the British government that controlled the Gold Coast. Kofi's father, Henry, continued the family's role of leadership as an elected governor of the Ashanti province and as a hereditary noble of the Fante people. Meanwhile, Kofi's mother, Victoria, followed a traditional lifestyle, caring for Kofi and his twin sister, Efua.

Henry was a quiet, strong father who, like many of the Fante people, was well educated, hardworking, and open-minded. In later years, when Henry took a job with an industrial corporation, he made sure that Kofi and the rest of his family were always aware of two different worlds at the same time. Kofi learned about his Fante heritage, with its deep roots in African culture, and also about the American and European business world beyond Kumasi. "My family moved in and out all the time from a traditional to a modern urban setting," Kofi would remember later.

Local ethnic concerns and broad global issues were equally important in the Annan household. As a result, Kofi developed an understanding of his people—and of the world—at an early age.

THE GOLD COAST COLONY

In 1938, when Kofi was born, the Gold Coast was a British colony rich in natural resources. It was the source of considerable wealth for the British Empire. The Gold Coast had been created in the

1800s, when Great Britain, along with other European countries, took over Africa, divided the continent into colonies, and put the African people to work in order to increase European wealth.

The cocoa plant, the source of chocolate, was the Gold Coast colony's most important export. But the land was also rich in tin, diamonds, and gold. Although the African people of the colony did most of the farming and mining, much of the profits from their work went to the British Empire. Before

One of the world's largest gold mines is in the Gold Coast (now Ghana), where Kofi Annan was born in 1938.

long, the African people, including many Fante, were protesting the unfairness of this system.

By the time Kofi Annan was born, the Gold Coast was moving slowly but surely toward independence from colonial rule. In the early 1900s, African intellectuals in the Gold Coast were talking about nationalism—the idea of an independent and free nation—and making progress toward their goal. In 1930, delegates from one nationalist group, the Gold Coast Youth Conference, traveled to London to ask British officials to govern more fairly.

But the British officials did not move quickly enough to satisfy the nationalists. In 1937, a year before Kofi Annan's birth, the people of the Gold Coast organized a strike known as the "cocoa hold-up." The cocoa farmers refused to hand over their crop to British companies and the companies lost money. To end the strike of the cocoa farmers, colonial officials were forced to create better, fairer trading laws. The cocoa hold-up and the resulting agreements were the first major steps toward the Gold Coast's freedom.

THE BIRTH OF THE UNITED NATIONS

Then, in 1939, a year after Kofi's birth, World War II (1939–1945) began. Germany under the Nazi Party of Adolf Hitler, Italy under the Fascist

Party of Benito Mussolini, and Japan under the aggressive rule of Prime Minister Hideki Tojo, banded together and invaded weaker nations all over the world. Great Britain, joined in 1941 by the United States and the Soviet Union, fought as Allies. In August 1941, Prime Minister Winston Churchill of Britain and President Franklin D. Roosevelt of the United States met in the Atlantic Ocean aboard a British warship and issued a joint declaration called the Atlantic Charter.

Among the ideals the Allies supported in the Atlantic Charter was "the right of all peoples to choose the form of government under which they will live." By allowing people to choose their own governments, the Atlantic Charter suggested an end to the colonial system. In January 1942, twenty-six Allied nations signed a document called the Declaration of the United Nations. This was the first official use of the term *United Nations*, which had been first used by Roosevelt. During the course of the war, twenty-one more nations added their signatures to the declaration.

Then, in 1945, after the Allies won the war, representatives from fifty nations gathered in San Francisco, California, to draft a charter for the United Nations—an organization designed to give the nations of the world a place to discuss their differences without resorting to violence. Under the UN Charter, which went into effect on October 24, 1945, colonies could appear before the UN member nations to complain about unfair treatment. Once again, colonial rule in places such as the Gold Coast seemed destined to end.

Winston Churchill of Britain (in black) and President Franklin D. Roosevelt (with cane) at the Atlantic Charter meeting

The UN Charter was signed in 1945.

AN INDEPENDENT GHANA

After the success of the cocoa hold-up, and with the Atlantic Charter and the UN Charter fresh in their minds, Gold Coast nationalists renewed their efforts for freedom. Some of the efforts turned violent, and Great Britain's "model colony" of peaceful, well-educated, hardworking Africans erupted in riots between nationalists and colonial forces.

Finally, in 1951, the British were forced to give up some of their power, and they called a general election. In the election, the people of the Gold Coast selected Kwame Nkrumah—a leader of mass action strikes and boycotts who had been jailed by the British for his nationalist work. Nkrumah, who had been educated in the United States and England, shared his governing duties with the British until 1957, when the Gold Coast finally won complete independence.

The people of the Gold Coast renamed the nation the Republic of Ghana, and it became the first colony of central and southern Africa to win its freedom from the Europeans. Other European colonies such as Nigeria in Africa and many in Southeast Asia became independent nations following Ghana's success. By 1960, seventeen of these former colonies had joined the United Nations as independent states.

Through much of the 1950s, young Kofi Annan watched the independence movement from the safety of a boarding school and later from the University of Science and Technology in his home city of Kumasi. He was too young to take part in the real struggles of the day, though he did organize a hunger strike among students, refusing to eat until the school administrators created a bet-

Kwame Nkrumah, leader of the Gold Coast, waves to celebrating crowds after winning independence from Britain in 1957.

ter menu. However, the boy who was taught to appreciate both traditional and modern ways learned an important lesson from Nkrumah's nationalist movement. He later explained, "As a teenager, as a young man, I saw major changes taking place around me. The colonial power was

Kofi Annan (top row, second from left) attended boarding school in Ghana.

handed over to the country, to what we call 'freedom fighters.' People were released from jail and became prime ministers and presidents. So I grew up believing that change is possible, that everything is possible, that one can dare to try to make a difference. That spirit is helpful. One is not easily intimidated or impressed by threats."

> **"I grew up believing that change is possible, that everything is possible, that one can dare to try to make a difference."**

CHAPTER TWO

AN AMERICAN EDUCATION

At the University of Science and Technology in Kumasi, Kofi developed a keen appreciation for the complicated world around him. Of course, for all his natural intelligence, he was not yet the shrewd observer he would become later in life. As he remembered in one of his favorite stories, he still had a lot to learn: "One day the headmaster walked into the classroom and he put up a broad white sheet of paper, about one meter by one meter, with a small black dot in the corner. And he asked, 'Boys, what do you see?' And all of us shouted in unison, 'A black dot!' And he stood back and said, 'So not a single one of you saw the broad white sheet of paper? Don't go through life with that attitude.' "

That lesson—the importance of seeing and understanding the larger picture—is one that Kofi would return to often in the years to come.

And he had an opportunity to test this skill almost immediately.

A CHANCE TO STUDY ABROAD

During the 1958–1959 school year, Kofi served as vice president of the national student union, an organization of students from all over Ghana. As vice president, Kofi attracted the attention of the Ford Foundation.

This charitable organization, founded in 1936 with donations from automakers Henry and Edsel Ford, seeks to promote peace, human welfare, and the preservation of the environment. The foundation was impressed with Kofi's intelligence and leadership qualities. Through its Foreign Students Leadership Project, Kofi won a scholarship to attend university in the United States for a year. With the support of the Ford Foundation, he was encouraged to enter the larger world he had always admired from the safety of Kumasi.

Before beginning his year of study, Kofi traveled to the United States to attend a summer program at Harvard University in Cambridge, Massachusetts. After adjusting to U.S. culture and teaching methods that summer, he headed inland to the city of St. Paul, Minnesota, home of Macalester College.

A college scholarship brought Kofi Annan to the United States in 1959.

LIFE IN MINNESOTA

At Macalester College, the faculty emphasized the importance of world peace and international fellowship (the UN flag flew alongside the U.S. flag on all Macalester flagposts) and taught their students to be good world citizens. Kofi blossomed there. In 1960, he served as president of the Cosmopolitan Club, which encouraged friendly rela-

As president of the Cosmopolitan Club at Macalester College, Kofi Annan explains his native Ghanaian dress to fellow students at a school event.

tions between United States citizens and international students. He also won a Minnesota public-speaking contest and set a school record in the 60-yard dash.

Kofi adjusted to life in the United States remarkably well. It took a little while, however, for the young man born and raised in the tropical climate of northwest Africa to adjust to the cold, wet weather of Minnesota. Now he had to learn how to shovel snow, layer his clothing, and wear a scarf, though at first he refused to wear earmuffs. "I resisted as long as I could," he remembers, "until one day, going to get something to eat, my ears nearly froze. So I went and bought the biggest pair I could find. But even in that I learned a very important lesson. You never walk into a situation and believe that you know better than the natives. You have to listen and look around. Otherwise, you can make some very serious mistakes."

American football, a game he had never played in Ghana, was even harder for him to accept. "It was OK as long as I kept running and no one caught up with me," he remembered of his first football practice. "Otherwise, I was like a piece of paper—I weighed 138 pounds, and that's not football weight. So I gave it up after fifteen minutes." Kofi chose to play on the college soccer team instead.

In spite of his problems with earmuffs and football, Kofi became a popular figure on the Macalester campus, remembered fondly by his classmates. "Kofi was usually quiet," recalled his teammate from the debate team Jack Mason. "But he had a self-deprecating sense of humor and an inner strength that commanded respect."

THE CIVIL RIGHTS MOVEMENT

The ability to rely on inner strength would be important to Kofi during his short stay at Macalester, as it was to African-Americans all over the United States at that time. After centuries of racism and oppression, first under a system of slavery and later under a system of legalized segregation, or separation of the races,

At Macalester, Kofi Annan (center) played on the soccer team.

African-Americans were just beginning another difficult phase in their struggle for equality—the Civil Rights movement.

Since the early 1950s, prominent African-Americans had been fighting segregation in the nation's courts and protesting against it on the streets. Sometimes stirring up violence, always creating publicity and outrage, the Civil Rights

During Kofi Annan's time at Macalester, the Civil Rights movement and its leader Martin Luther King Jr. (shown leading demonstrators down a Georgia street) were often in the news.

movement was gaining power just as Kofi Annan was finishing his studies at Macalester.

The struggle of African-Americans in the early 1960s seemed familiar to Kofi, who had just seen the people of his own country fight for equality. "It was an exciting period. I had come from Ghana and we had just gone through our own struggle for independence," he remembered years later. "When I came to the States, the social upheaval reminded me of some things that had gone on in Ghana."

With the success of Ghana's independence movement fresh in his mind, Kofi was more optimistic about the Civil Rights movement than were his African-American friends. He knew that change of all kinds was possible.

But even he became discouraged at times. In the United States, the color of his skin put him in danger. For example, in an incident that earned a personal apology from the mayor of Minneapolis, Kofi was almost assaulted by a white gang while he was walking with a white girl in the city.

Even though Kofi was himself a target of racist violence, his faith in people and their ability to change never faltered. Similarly, his memories of his time at Macalester never suffered: "There was a celebration of diversity throughout this student body unlike any other I have known. . . . Students from a wide range of backgrounds and nationalities lived, worked, and grew together. We were not merely greeted with tolerance, we were welcomed with warmth."

TOURING THE UNITED STATES

At Macalester, the students worked hard to build that sense of tolerance and warmth. During the summer of 1960, Kofi and four other students piled into a station wagon with Professor Henry Morgan and toured the United States. The students—Kofi from Ghana, one boy from Great Britain, one from Greece, one from Sri Lanka, and one from the United States—called themselves the Ambassadors for Friendship. Their goal was to see as much of the country as they could from as many perspectives as possible.

The group stayed with rich families and poor families and once even tried to stay in the jailhouse in Dodge City, Kansas, just to see the conditions. The jailer claimed it was the first time in his thirty-two-year career that anyone wanted to be locked up, and he refused to let the boys in. Undaunted, they stayed at the local Salvation Army shelter instead.

Of course they confronted some racism along the way—the Sri Lankan boy, for instance, wasn't allowed to use the hotel pool in Las Vegas. But

Kofi Annan (second from left) was a member of a college student group called the Ambassadors for Friendship.

Kofi ultimately came away from the trip believing that American people were generous. And that trip with the Ambassadors for Friendship was the beginning of his long and complicated relationship with the United States, one he would reevaluate frequently in later years.

GRADUATION AND BEYOND

In 1961, Kofi received his bachelor of arts degree in economics from Macalester and was looking forward to the beginning of his adult life. Of course, he had no idea what life held for him. He assumed that his future would somehow be intertwined with his homeland of Ghana: "I figured that after my schooling, I would make some money in the business world, then I would—at, say, forty-five—enter politics in Ghana and help develop the country. And at sixty I would retire to become a farmer. And I would die at eighty in bed. But it's one of those things God does. Our most intricate plans don't always turn out as we expected."

> **"I figured . . . at sixty I would retire to become a farmer. . . . Our most intricate plans don't always turn out as we expected."**

Indeed there were many surprises in store for Kofi Annan. His life would take on a greater significance than he could ever have expected.

CHAPTER THREE

SOMETHING FOR MANKIND

Leaving Macalester in 1961 as a college graduate with a promising future in newly independent Ghana, Kofi Annan was still not satisfied that he had learned enough to make his mark in the world. Convinced of the importance of an extensive education, he decided to go back to school rather than enter the business world. This time, he headed for Europe and worked toward a graduate degree in economics at the Institut Universitaire des Hautes Etudes Internationales (the Graduate Institute of International Studies) in Geneva, Switzerland.

Once again, Annan threw himself into a foreign culture. This time, it was a mountainous country in the Alps where the people spoke mostly German, Italian, and French. In some ways, Geneva was very different from the United States he had come to know so well. And it was certainly very different from Ghana. But Annan adapted to his new environment with relative ease and completed his studies by 1962.

A DIFFICULT DECISION

As he was preparing to leave Geneva, Kofi Annan had to make a difficult decision. Although he had planned to go home to Ghana after graduation, he

Kofi Annan attended graduate school in Geneva, Switzerland, in the 1960s.

now had second thoughts. His best opportunity in Ghana—a job with Pillsbury, a food company—seemed to be a dead end. And the political situation in Ghana seemed less stable than it had a few years earlier.

The nation was once again tangled in political crisis. After setting up a democratic government and skillfully leading Ghana through the early years of independence, President Kwame Nkrumah was taking more and more power for himself. Finally, in 1966, a military council ousted Nkrumah and suspended Ghana's constitution. But even in 1962, there were signs that peace in Ghana was falling apart. And Kofi Annan was anxious to start his career without feeling threatened by the turmoil in his homeland.

Nkrumah was responsible for the increasing unrest in Ghana in the early 1960s, but he was also responsible for a change that inspired young Kofi—the independence of Africa from European colonial rule. In 1958, after Nkrumah and his supporters succeeded in freeing Ghana from British rule, he announced that Ghana's independence was "meaningless, unless it is linked up with the total liberation of Africa."

Gathering the former colonies and new nations of the continent into alliances, Nkrumah succeeded in 1963 in establishing the Organiza-

In 1963, President Kwame Nkrumah of Ghana organized a group of African states called the Organization of African Unity.

tion of African Unity. This group included the existing thirty-two African states. Suddenly, after centuries of dependence on Europe, the governments of Africa were cooperating with one another and governing themselves.

A JOB AT THE UNITED NATIONS

With excitement running high about the independence movements in Ghana and the rest of the African continent, and with the lessons he learned at Macalester College still fresh in his mind, Annan decided to take a job with the United Nations in 1962. He stayed in Geneva and became an administrative and budget officer for the World Health Organization (WHO), a UN agency. WHO is dedicated to improving health standards around the world, one of the sixteen UN agencies that seek to improve living conditions and promote peace among nations.

As an administrative officer, Kofi Annan originally held one of the lowest jobs in the entire organization, but he was capable of much more. Annan soon worked his way up, relying on his economic expertise for promotions in the budget department and, later, at the Economic Commission for Africa, which helped to stabilize the governments and economies of developing nations such as Ghana.

A PERFECT FIT

For Kofi Annan—a product of the Ghanaian independence movement, the U.S. Civil Rights movement, and the international emphasis of Macalester College—the United Nations was exactly the right place to be in 1962. Already sensitive to local as well as global problems, Annan fit perfectly into the UN community. And he was now an employee of the organization once headed by his role model, Dag Hammarskjöld.

Hammarskjöld had been Sweden's vice minister of foreign affairs before becoming the UN secretary-general in 1953. He directed UN activity during a time known as the Cold War—a dangerous era when the United States and the Soviet Union were competing for world power. The two nations resented UN interference in their plans, but Hammarskjöld was not timid in his dealings with the superpowers. He was a strong leader and a supporter of peace in troubled times. He eventually died on a peace mission, when his airplane crashed in Africa during war negotiations in Congo in 1961.

Kofi Annan, completing his last year at Macalester when Hammarskjöld died, had no idea that he would be working for the United Nations within two years. But he would always remember

As a young man, Kofi Annan always admired Dag Hammarskjöld, whose portrait hangs in the lobby of UN Headquarters.

the secretary-general's last public statement as an important lesson. Hammarskjöld said: "It is false pride to boast to the world about the importance of one's work, but it is false humility, and finally just as destructive, not to recognize—and recognize with gratitude—that one's work has a sense. . . . Let us work in the conviction that our work has a meaning beyond the narrow and individual one and has meant something for man[kind]."

Now an employee of the United Nations, Kofi Annan truly believed that he was following Hammarskjöld's advice. He was doing work that "meant something for mankind."

CHAPTER FOUR

A RISING STAR

Kofi Annan took a year off from his UN duties in 1971 to attend classes at the Massachusetts Institute of Technology (MIT), where he earned a master of science degree in management. By 1972, Annan seemed to be living a relatively happy, comfortable life. He was married to a Nigerian woman (though they would later divorce). He was the father of a little girl, Ana, and soon to be the father of a boy, Kojo. He was also back in New York City, holding an administrative position at UN Headquarters in Manhattan.

A BRIEF RETURN TO GHANA

But then Annan decided it was time for a change. After nearly a decade of hard work with the United Nations, he wanted to pursue his original goal—to find a way to improve conditions in

Kofi Annan talks to fellow MIT students in Cambridge, Massachusetts, during his time there in 1971.

Ghana. In 1974, he wrapped up his work in New York and headed back to his homeland, this time as managing director of the Ghana Tourist Development Company.

Ghana was still bogged down in political conflict, as the government shifted between military and civilian rule. As a tourism official, however, Annan found himself in a unique position to attract foreigners to Ghana. And, along with the foreigners came some much-needed money. While promoting tourism programs, he also served on the Ghana Tourist Control Board, working with the government to improve Ghana's future.

Although he was successful in his new position, Annan soon realized that his ties to the United Nations were strong, maybe even stronger than his ties to Ghana. He respected the work the UN was doing for people all over the world and he enjoyed being part of that work. So in 1976, Annan left Ghana once again to return to Geneva and the UN community.

BACK IN GENEVA

In 1980, he was made deputy director of administration and head of personnel for the United Nations High Commission for Refugees (UNHCR) in Geneva. Refugees are people who have been forced out of their homes because of war, prejudice, or famine. Homeless and impoverished, refugees often need help finding food, shelter, and medicine. UNHCR works to protect refugees from violence, provide for their needs, and helps them with their problems.

When Annan began his work with UNHCR, there were 8 million refugees around the world—including 5 million in his native Africa. Annan was in charge of the large UNHCR staff assembled to assist so many refugees. As usual, he was known throughout the high commission for his efficiency, his organizational skills, and his calming influence.

A ROMANCE

Among the people Annan charmed at UNHCR was a woman named Nane Lagergren, a former Swedish judge working as a UNHCR lawyer in Geneva. Nane caught Annan's eye in 1981, and their romance began shortly thereafter.

Both Kofi and Nane had been divorced and Nane, like Kofi, was a parent (Nane's daughter, Nina, was born in 1970). Also like Kofi, Nane came from a distinguished family. Her mother's half-brother was the heroic Raoul Wallenberg, a Swedish diplomat and humanitarian who had mysteriously disappeared in 1945 while rescuing Jewish people from Hitler's Nazis and the genocide of the Holocaust. Wallenberg was another of Annan's role models.

In 1981, as his relationship with Nane blossomed, Annan took on an extra job, becoming governor of the UN International School in Geneva—the school their children, Ana, Kojo, and Nina, were attending. In 1984, Kofi and Nane were married in a ceremony held at the UN chapel in New York.

Kofi with his wife, Nane

Leaving her law practice behind, Nane moved with Kofi to Roosevelt Island, a small community on the East River near Manhattan. Annan became director of the budget in the UN Office of Financial Services in New York, while Nane devoted most of her time to painting. The newlyweds were extremely happy together, though they had to work through some cultural differences early on, as Annan remembers: "At the beginning it was very difficult. We would organize a dinner. Nane, being a Swede . . . was used to punctuality. But the Ghanaian or the African guests would come about thirty minutes to an hour late, and she used to get furious." Cultural differences aside, however, Kofi and Nane created a strong partnership together.

Annan's talent for economic problem-solving and his great patience served him well in his role as budget director, but Javier Perez de Cuellar, UN secretary-general from 1982 to 1991, saw further. He recognized that Annan's experience and talents could be put to even greater use. So in 1987, Perez de Cuellar appointed Annan assistant secretary-general in the Office of Human Resources Management. In this position, Annan became staff director for the entire United Nations at a crucial time in the history of the twentieth century.

Secretary-General Javier Perez de Cuellar appointed Annan assistant secretary-general in 1987.

THE END OF THE COLD WAR

Cold War tensions between the United States and the former Soviet Union were decreasing and Perez de Cuellar was successfully negotiating peace in war-torn countries such as Afghanistan, Iran, Namibia, Nicaragua, and El Salvador. By 1988, UN projects were successful in so many areas of the world that UN peacekeepers were collectively awarded the Nobel Prize for peace.

And then in 1989 came the collapse of the Communist bloc—the political alliance that included several Eastern European nations as well as the Soviet Union. Supporters of democratic government throughout Eastern Europe protested against Soviet domination. They dismantled the infamous Berlin Wall, which had once divided Germany's most important city into communist and democratic halves. The Cold War—one of the most tense periods in modern history—was over.

A CHALLENGE FOR ANNAN

The end of the Cold War did not usher in a period of world peace, however. In August 1990, Iraqi leader Saddam Hussein invaded neighboring Kuwait. Since so much of the world's fuel originates in and around Kuwait and the Persian Gulf, the invasion signaled a worldwide crisis. The United States and its allies quickly prepared their armies for war. But as the nations chose sides and prepared to fight, thousands of foreigners, including UN workers, were trapped in Iraq and Kuwait with no way of returning home.

Perez de Cuellar appointed Annan to head the negotiations for the release of UN workers stranded behind Iraqi lines. After almost thirty years in the UN organization, Annan was finally given a major task to perform on the international stage.

As always, he was relatively calm on the eve of his first major diplomatic mission. But when an aide asked him for a backup plan if the Iraqis refused to release the UN workers, Annan snapped back, "Don't ever speak to me negatively when I'm about to negotiate. We'll make it—and I don't want to hear that we may not make it." For the people behind Iraqi lines, Annan's mission was a matter of life and death, and the diplomat knew what was at stake.

> **"Don't ever speak to me negatively when I'm about to negotiate."**

In the end, he negotiated the safe return of all 900 UN workers as well as arranging for the eventual release of 500,000 Asians who were also stranded in the warring nations. For the United Nations and for Annan, the negotiations were an extraordinary triumph. And it would not be Annan's last.

CHAPTER FIVE

THE PEACEKEEPER

Following his successful diplomatic mission in Iraq, and with the world at war once again in the Persian Gulf, Kofi Annan was given a new job. In 1990, Perez de Cuellar put him back on the financial end of UN operations as assistant secretary-general for program planning, budget and finance. But as his diplomatic efforts proved, he was far too talented in international politics to stay in this business position for long. Soon enough, he would be assigned to a new diplomatic mission.

HARD TIMES FOR THE UNITED NATIONS

The United Nations was about to face one of the most difficult periods in its history. Enthusiasm over the fall of the Soviet Union and the end of the Cold War quickly evaporated as a new kind of struggle began to dominate international politics. Instead of large-scale wars between nations, regional conflicts between feuding ethnic groups erupted all over the world. These ethnic groups were competing for religious dominance, political dominance, or land. They did not operate according to established diplomatic rules and they had little regard for the United Nations.

Making matters worse, the United States—now the wealthiest and most powerful nation in the world—was refusing to invest as much money and as many workers in the organization as it had in the past. At a time when small regional wars were increasing, the United States was abandoning the organization it had helped to create, criticizing the United Nations for being expensive and unsuccessful.

Secretary-General Javier Perez de Cuellar's term of office expired in 1991 and the UN General Assembly elected former university professor and Egyptian minister of state Boutros Boutros-Ghali to take Perez de Cuellar's place. Boutros-Ghali immediately understood the enormity of his task as a diplomat in an age of scattered, regional conflicts: "Never before in its history has the United Nations been so action-oriented, so actively engaged and so widely expected to respond to needs both immediate and pervasive."

ANNAN THE PEACEKEEPER

On March 1, 1993, Boutros-Ghali appointed Kofi Annan undersecretary-general for peacekeeping operations. In effect, Annan became the person in charge of the UN response to the "immediate" and "pervasive" demands of world conflict. He was asked to monitor all the world's violent struggles and devise strategies for restoring peace.

Undersecretary-General Annan reports to Boutros Boutros-Ghali, the sixth UN secretary-general, on peacekeeping operations around the world.

When Annan began this work, there were seventeen separate peacekeeping operations worldwide, each with its own staff and troops. The UN peacekeeping troops, gathered from the armies of member nations, are known as "blue berets" after the powder-blue berets or helmets they wear. Their duties range from protecting voting places during democratic elections to protecting endangered peoples around the globe. In all situations, the UN peacekeepers are expected to be neutral and preserve peace without taking sides.

PEACE EFFORTS IN AFRICA

In 1993, Annan's abilities as a peacekeeper were tested in the east African nation of Somalia. A few months after he accepted his new post, political tensions in that war-torn, famine-stricken country were again spilling into the streets of the capital city of Mogadishu.

A U.S.-led military force had been trying to restore order in Mogadishu since the end of 1992, but after the United States pulled its troops out in 1993, supporters of Somali warlord Mohammed Farah Aidid attacked and murdered a number of the remaining UN peacekeepers. The UN nations were outraged by the killings but did not want to lose any more soldiers. Annan was forced to withdraw all UN peacekeepers from Somalia in 1995.

Although thirty Americans and ninety-one UN soldiers died during the Somali operations, Aidid continued to keep a stranglehold on the economy of the country. It marked a significant failure in UN history. In addition, the United States and its allies, disappointed by the failures

Annan, under pressure from UN nations, pulled UN troops out of Mogadishu, Somalia, in 1995.

of the UN in Somalia, were even more hesitant to contribute to other peacekeeping missions. As a result, when ethnic conflict between the Hutu and Tutsi peoples of the central African nation of Rwanda exploded into a horrifically violent war in 1994, Annan's department had little support and was powerless to halt the slaughter.

People watching the Somali and Rwandan crises on television were shocked by the violence. As peacekeeping official Shashi Tharoor remembers, many nations begged the UN to help stop the killing: "The news media shows us a situation in a manner that clamors for international response. So as the world says, 'Don't just stand there. Do something!' the UN is obliged to consider what it can do."

But there was little Annan and his department could do when the United States and its allies withdrew support—both money and troops—for the peacekeeping missions. The feeling of powerlessness began to frustrate and sadden Annan: "One time, during the beginning of the Somalia crisis, I went to walk in the woods with my phone. It rang, and I picked up, giving some instructions. Then I walked some more. After a while, I could hear the phone trying to ring. I looked down at the phone and it said 'low battery.' I thought [pointing to his heart], this battery is low too."

POSITIVE CHANGES

Even though he was discouraged by recent events, Annan pushed forward with a number of changes in the peacekeeping organization. He increased the number of peacekeeping troops worldwide from 11,500 in 1992 to 72,000 in 1994, set up a computerized, 24-hour "Situation Center" to monitor world crises, and established a "Lessons Learned Unit" to analyze UN peacekeeping results.

By the end of 1994, Annan was becoming a well-known figure in the international community. Macalester College presented him with a Trustee Distinguished Service Award honoring his thirty years of service to the international community.

FIGHTING IN BOSNIA

The worst conflict in Annan's tenure as undersecretary-general for peacekeeping operations was just beginning, however. After the fall of the Soviet Union in 1991, the Eastern European nation of Yugoslavia crumbled, breaking into parts roughly divided along ethnic lines: Bosnia-Herzegovina, Serbia, Croatia, Slovenia, and Macedonia. However, the ethnic lines were not always the same as the political lines. Not all Serbs lived within the boundaries of Serbia, for example, and not all Bosnians lived in Bosnia. In the early 1990s, ethnic Serbs in Bosnia began a campaign of "ethnic cleansing," designed to wipe out the Muslim people of Bosnia and take their land.

In 1992, the United Nations sent thousands of blue berets into Bosnia to end the fighting and maintain a cease-fire while the warring parties negotiated a settlement. The cease-fire was repeatedly ignored, however, and the fighting continued.

In March 1993, just after taking control of peacekeeping operations, Annan struggled to find a new peace agreement acceptable to the warring parties and to the United States and its allies. Once again, the nations of the world refused to provide Annan with more peacekeeping troops, but Annan was determined to preserve what was left of Bosnia. "The UN is the only world policeman today," he said, begging for international support. "When the superpowers were around, they shared [power] with us. Now the Russians are gone and the Americans have no stomach for playing policeman." Given the poor international response to his call, eight cease-fires in Bosnia failed and more people were killed.

Disgusted with the developments in Bosnia, Boutros-Ghali asked Annan to take over for the United Nation's Bosnia representative—Yasushi Akashi—in late 1993. But Annan could not influence events in Bosnia without international backing—and the killing continued.

Finally, in 1995, President Bill Clinton called the leaders of Bosnia, Serbia, and Croatia to the negotiating table in Dayton, Ohio. Following the peace agreement the leaders hammered out in Dayton, the UN withdrew its troops from Bosnia, leaving a U.S.-backed force in its place. Annan oversaw the transfer of power.

Kofi Annan with the commander of the U.S.-backed NATO mission (left) and the leader of the UN peacekeepers (right) during the official transfer of power in Bosnia in 1995

NATO TAKES OVER IN BOSNIA

While Kofi Annan hoped that a lasting peace would still be possible in Bosnia, he knew that the world had once again failed to prevent a catastrophe. As he handed over the UN mission to the North Atlantic Treaty Organization (NATO), a military alliance of the United States and its allies, he delivered one of the most memorable speeches of his career: "The world cannot claim ignorance of what those who live here have endured. In looking back, we should all recall how we responded to the escalating horrors of the last four years. And, as we do, there are questions which each of us must ask: What did I do? Could I have done more? Did I let my prejudice, or my fear, overwhelm my reasoning? And, above all, how would I react next time?"

In gracefully surrendering control of Bosnia, Annan once again impressed world leaders with his diplomatic skill. As one U.S. official remembered, "He is the only top official of the UN who came out of the Bosnia experience with dignity and without having harmed the organization or [its] relations with any one of the great powers. That's what being a great diplomat's about."

In 1995, after struggling through almost three years of constant conflict, Annan was asked by the elders of the Fante people in the Akwamu region of Ghana if he would become their paramount chief. It is the highest honor the Fante people can bestow on an individual. As great an honor as the chieftanship was, and as much as Annan loved his homeland and his people, he declined the offer. To many people in the United Nations, it looked as if Annan was preparing to become the leader of a much larger organization.

CHAPTER SIX

THE TOP JOB

By the end of his first five-year term as secretary-general, Boutros Boutros-Ghali had made enough enemies among world leaders that his reelection in 1996 seemed unlikely. Often acting more like a university professor than a diplomat, Boutros-Ghali angered many leaders. He lectured them about international politics, scolded them when they failed to carry out his plans, and suggested that the United States and its allies were responsible for the disasters in Somalia and Rwanda. Whether or not the accusations were true, Boutros-Ghali's approach to diplomacy was unpopular. Many diplomats were demanding a change in UN leadership.

UN POLITICS

In 1996, the UN elections coincided with U.S. presidential elections. President Bill Clinton, also seeking reelection, was hesitant to discuss Boutros-Ghali's unpopularity in public. Members of the U.S. Congress made the United Nations an issue in the presidential campaign, however, demanding that Clinton oppose Boutros-Ghali's reelection. They also called for other reforms to deal with the problems of too many UN workers, too much UN interference in world affairs, and above all, too much reliance on the United States for peacekeeping operations. In the five years since Boutros-Ghali had been elected, the members of Congress said, the United States had invested too much too many times in UN missions that had failed.

So Boutros-Ghali was now a "lame duck," a leader who has little power because he will not be in power much longer. Although the secretary-general had achieved the first democratic elections in the nations of Cambodia and Mozambique, he had also watched the eruption of violence in Somalia, Rwanda, Bosnia, Haiti, and Angola. Even if the U.S. criticism was unfair, no one believed Boutros-Ghali would be reelected, so world leaders began to search for a replacement. Among the candidates considered were Gareth Evans, Australia's foreign minister; Mary Robinson, the president of Ireland; and Gro Harlem Bruntland, the prime minister of Norway.

In the end, the most popular candidates came

from Africa, a continent that was relying heavily on UN economic and military support. Anara Essy, foreign minister of the Ivory Coast, was the early favorite. He was especially popular with France and its closest allies because he spoke French fluently. But as the UN elections drew closer, Essy faced stiff competition from the candidate endorsed by the United States and many other nations—Kofi Annan.

A NEW JOB FOR ANNAN

In mid-December, Annan was clearly pulling ahead in the race for the UN's top office. And on December 17, 1996, over protests by French delegates, Annan was elected secretary-general. He was the first UN leader to have risen through the ranks of the organization and the first man from black Africa to hold this major international office.

The boy from Ghana, who began his career near the bottom of the UN organization, was now at the top. Serving a term beginning on January 1, 1997, and ending on December 31, 2001, he would also be the first secretary-general of the twenty-first century. In his acceptance speech, Annan expressed his determination to lead a United Nations that would be a strong force for peace in the world: "Applaud us when we prevail;

Secretary-General Kofi Annan acknowledges a standing ovation from the UN staff at UN Headquarters after his appointment.

correct us when we fail; but, above all, do not let this indispensable, irreplaceable institution wither, languish, or perish as a result of member state indifference, inattention, or financial starvation."

Annan's message was clear. Without the financial and military support of every nation, the UN would be powerless to change the course of world events. Like Boutros-Ghali before him,

Annan was certain that peace among the 185 member nations of the United Nations would be impossible if all nations did not play an active role in UN projects. "I have 185 masters," Annan was fond of saying, and he was going to try to bring all 185 nations into his decisions.

At the postelection celebration, Annan looked as cool and calm as usual, though his friends noticed that he kept shifting his weight from one foot to the other. "That's what he does when he shows emotion," observed one UN employee. Annan had plenty to be both excited and nervous about. As secretary-general, he was the coordinator of a UN worldwide staff of more than 10,000 people.

In addition, he was to give a yearly report to the General Assembly—the congress of representatives from every UN member nation. He would speak about the progress his organization was making in preserving world peace and relieving problems such as famine and economic instability. Perhaps the most important responsibility of all was outlined in Article 99 of the UN Charter, the document that describes the rules and procedures of the UN. The secretary-general is responsible for bringing issues that threaten international peace and security to the attention of the UN Security Council, the decision-making board of powerful nations within the organization.

A POPULAR LEADER

Few people who knew Annan or his record with the United Nations doubted his ability to run an effective organization. Madeleine Albright, then U.S. ambassador to the United Nations and later U.S. secretary of state, was instrumental in getting Annan the top job. Other workers within the United Nations were thrilled that Annan, a veteran of international diplomacy and a person who had held jobs at every level of the organization, was now their boss. He had earned their undivided loyalty. And even people such as Roger Mosvick, Annan's communication studies professor at Macalester, also spoke up in support of the new secretary-general: "He can understand not only the problems and grievances of underdeveloped nations, he also understands the positions of the [wealthier nations]. That makes him a very honest broker."

As part of the new job, Annan received a $300,000-per-year salary and the use of the secretary-general's house, a nineteenth-century mansion on Sutton Place near the East River in Manhattan. From that base of operations, Annan set out to transform the office of secretary-general.

While his predecessor, Boutros-Ghali, failed to charm world leaders, Annan has an easy, friendly manner and people feel comfortable in his

The residence of the secretary-general is located on Sutton Place, in New York City.

company. With Nane by his side, his youthfulness and vitality make him a favorite among the artists, publishers, executives, and celebrities in New York City and around the world. And this popularity puts Annan in a unique position among secretaries-general to affect change in the world. "If I can't get the support of governments,"

Annan says, "then I'll get the support of the people. People move governments."

THE ANNAN ADMINISTRATION

To help him in his new position, Annan put together a prestigious cabinet of advisors, including international diplomats well known for their experience and knowledge of world affairs. The cabinet was a new idea in UN administration. Annan was careful to choose advisors who would be respected around the globe and would in turn respect the responsibilities of their new assignments.

Canadian diplomat Louise Frechette was appointed deputy secretary-general. Mary Robinson, the former president of Ireland, became high commissioner for human rights. Pino Arlacchi, an Italian expert on organized crime, heads the UN war on drugs. And Gro Harlem Brundtland, the former prime minister of Norway, is director general of the World Health Organization. Annan and his cabinet together proposed to "demystify the United Nations and not make it so bureaucratic and distant from the average person. We should bring the organization closer to the people."

Annan with Mary Robinson, former president of Ireland, now high commissioner for human rights

But by January 1997, as he took up some of the biggest issues ever addressed by a secretary-general, Annan already knew that bringing the United Nations "closer to the people" would not be as easy as it sounded.

CHAPTER SEVEN

FOR A PEACEFUL FUTURE

As the newly elected secretary-general, Annan first turned his attention to central Africa, a region torn by ethnic conflict between two rival groups—the Hutu and the Tutsi. This ethnic conflict had been at the heart of the Rwanda crisis earlier in the decade. By 1996, however, the conflict had spilled over into the neighboring nation of Burundi and the large nation of Zaire.

Before becoming secretary-general, Annan had warned the world that the problems in Burundi would grow to unmanageable proportions. "We have to move very quickly before everything blows up in our faces," he announced in July. "As it is, history will judge us rather severely for Rwanda. I don't think we can repeat the experience in Burundi." His warning was ignored, however, and the ethnic conflict spread.

Then, in February 1997, Annan learned that

the UN International War Crimes Tribunal, a law court created to investigate genocide in Rwanda, was being mismanaged. The chief administrators of the court were misusing the court's money and discriminating against non-Africans in hiring. Annan acted quickly to fire the administrators and organize a new staff for the Rwandan court.

In his approach to African conflict, Annan proved that he had important things to say and that he wasn't afraid to act on his convictions. If world leaders thought that the even-tempered Annan was going to be a weak leader in world affairs, they were learning very quickly that they had been greatly mistaken.

REFORMING THE UNITED NATIONS

Annan's main task during the early months of his administration was to convince the nations of the world that he was willing to reform the UN organization. Although Boutros-Ghali had been accused of allowing the United Nations to grow too large, he had actually cut the UN staff by 3,000 during his term. However, in response to pressure from the world's poor nations to address their problems, Boutros-Ghali had created 700 new positions designed specifically to help those nations develop their economies. These new positions cost the wealthier nations an extra $122 mil-

*Kofi Annan at his desk at UN Headquarters
in New York*

lion per year. So in 1997, Annan found himself in
the delicate position of having to please two
opposing groups—the poor nations who needed
more help than they could pay for and the wealthy
nations who were expected to pay the bills.

Annan responded first by cutting an addi-
tional 1,000 jobs from the UN Secretariat—the
UN administrative staff. He consolidated twelve
departments into five and created a cabinet to

help him oversee all the UN functions. These reforms were known as Annan's "quiet revolution," but they were not enough to satisfy many of the wealthy nations, including the United States, which alone contributes 25 percent of the UN budget.

In fact, the U.S. government was so displeased with Annan's reforms that members of Congress refused to pay their UN bill of $1.3 billion, holding off on the payments until Annan made large-scale changes in UN management and policies. They were even willing to give up their voting rights in the decision-making Security Council and withdraw from the organization entirely by refusing to meet the January 1999 payment deadline.

NEGOTIATIONS IN IRAQ

With the pressure to be an effective, strong leader already growing, Annan faced his greatest trial early in 1998. Since the 1991 Persian Gulf War, the United States, with UN support, had been pressuring President Saddam Hussein of Iraq to give up his deadly chemical and biological weapons. Seven years later, Hussein was still refusing to cooperate with the UN weapons inspectors. President Clinton sent a number of aircraft carriers and troops to the Persian Gulf, once again threatening Hussein with war if he didn't cooperate.

This time, however, Russia, France, and China opposed the U.S. military threats. Many people in the United States also opposed Clinton's actions. With the threat of an unpopular war looming, Annan convinced Clinton that the United Nations should be allowed to negotiate a peace settlement.

After three days of secret talks, Annan left Iraq with a plan. Insisting that UN inspectors should continue their search for weapons of mass destruction, Annan agreed to create an economic program to ease the hardships caused by the UN trading restrictions against Iraq. Though most nations agreed not to trade with Iraq until Hussein cooperated with weapons inspections, Annan persuaded world leaders to accept an expanded "oil-for-food" program, which allowed Hussein to export more oil in order to earn money for food and medicine. By March 1998, President Clinton had approved the terms of Annan's negotiations.

AN INTERNATIONAL WAR COURT

Continuing to press ahead with his vision of a more powerful United Nations, Annan joined 150 nations in supporting the creation of a permanent International War Crimes Tribunal in The

Hague, the capital of the Netherlands. Based on the temporary war courts in Rwanda and Bosnia, the international tribunal would have the power to prosecute and punish those who violated human rights. The idea of a permanent court met opposition from the United States, France, China, and Russia, which all feared that such a court would give weaker nations an opportunity to legally attack stronger nations out of jealousy or resentment.

Annan stood firm in his support of the idea. "People all over the world want to know that humanity can strike back," he said in a speech that opened negotiations in June 1998. "That wherever and whenever genocide, war crimes, or other such violations are committed, there is a court before which the criminal can be held to account." Ultimately, over the objections of the four powerful nations, the tribunal was approved. Annan had scored yet another victory in his push for a more involved international community.

THE TASK AHEAD

Throughout its history, the United Nations has had relatively little success in brokering and preserving peace around the world. According to some estimates, the United Nations has achieved its goals in only 33 percent of the conflicts in which it has been involved.

Kofi Annan is not discouraged by the organization's troubled past, though. He sees a clear role for the United Nations in future world relations. He is quick to explain that the world now faces new threats to peace: "The greatest threat to

The challenges that face the United Nations and its leader, Kofi Annan, are great.

world stability today is crises like [those in] Rwanda and Somalia and Bosnia. It is not one of nuclear war . . . but rather a rising tide of ethnic and regional conflicts that could eventually engulf us all."

Annan's United Nations is also dedicated to the economic development of poor nations to help avoid ethnic and regional conflicts in the first place. "My aim is to get the UN and its agencies to work in a more focused, coordinated and cohesive manner to have greater impact . . . alleviating the poverty of those who live where [money] has not so far flowed," he has said.

The task ahead will be a difficult one for Kofi Annan. Eight of every ten people on the planet live in disadvantaged nations. Many of those people live in overcrowded cities where pollution and disease spread quickly. In addition, 43 million people worldwide have been forced from their homes due to war or prejudice in their homelands. These displaced peoples are often poor, and their problems strain the world economy.

Annan is determined to change this situation. His goals include helping poor nations build strong foundations, protecting displaced peoples, and convincing the wealthy nations of the world that they too have a stake in ending world poverty, discrimination, and warfare. "My sense is that we need the UN today perhaps more than ever. And despite the perception that the UN is under siege, I think the world is going to realize how much we need this organization. We need to ensure that we have the means to regulate relations among states, and we need to take on the whole range of issues that no country, no matter how powerful—even the United States—can deal with by itself, whether it's the environment, drugs, terrorism, health, or sustainable [economic] development."

Annan's task will be difficult. The problems of the modern world are not easy to solve and its leaders resist change. But world leaders and citizens are increasingly confident that Kofi Annan and the United Nations are making a positive difference in the ongoing struggle for world peace.

CHRONOLOGY

1938	Born on April 8 in the Gold Coast (now called Ghana)
1961	Earns a bachelor of arts degree in economics from Macalester College in St. Paul, Minnesota
1962	Graduates with a degree in economics from the Institut Universitaire des Hautes Etudes Internationales in Geneva, Switzerland; takes a job with the United Nations there
1972	Earns a master's degree in management at the Massachusetts Institute of Technology (MIT) in Cambridge, Massachusetts
1974	Takes a job as managing director of the Ghana Tourist Development Company in Ghana

1976	Returns to Geneva to work for the United Nations
1980	Promoted to deputy director of administration and head of personnel for the United Nations High Commission for Refugees (UNHCR) in Geneva
1984	Marries Nane Lagergren, a former Swedish judge, at the UN chapel in New York City
1987	Appointed assistant secretary-general in the Office of Human Resources Management by Javier Perez de Cuellar
1993	Appointed undersecretary-general for peacekeeping operations by Boutros Boutros-Ghali
1997	Began term as seventh secretary-general of the United Nations

THE SECRETARIES-GENERAL OF THE UNITED NATIONS

Secretary-General	Country	Term
Trygve Lie	Norway	(1946–1952)
Dag Hammarskjöld	Sweden	(1953–1961)
U Thant	Burma	(1962–1971)
Kurt Waldheim	Austria	(1972–1982)
Javier Perez de Cuellar	Peru	(1982–1991)
Boutros Boutros-Ghali	Egypt	(1992–1996)
Kofi Annan	Ghana	(1997–)

A NOTE ON SOURCES

In writing about the life of Kofi Annan, I faced several unusual challenges.

First, Annan was not a well-known figure until 1996, when he was elected secretary-general of the United Nations. Few journalists or historians had ever written anything about him before his name appeared on the list of possible candidates to succeed Javier Perez de Cuellar. No full-length biography of Annan had yet been published when I began my research.

Second, Annan has held the office of secretary-general for only a short time. Most writers prefer to write a story—whether fact or fiction—when they have some sense of how that story will end. In many ways, Kofi Annan's story is just beginning, so it is much more difficult to summarize.

Finally, when researching the life of a person who is still alive, biographers usually try to interview their subjects. Since Annan was not granting interviews, however, I had to rely on what had already been written about him.

As a result, I had to piece together Kofi Annan's life from a variety of sources. The most important were newspaper articles. The *New York Times* and the *Washington Post* feature particularly strong coverage of the United Nations. Reporters from both newspapers have gathered many important details about Annan's past and present. Now that articles from past issues are available on library Internet services such as Lexis-Nexis, newspapers are among the easiest sources for a biographer to use.

Magazine articles from past issues of *Newsweek*, *The New Yorker*, and *Macalester Today*, a magazine published by Macalester College, filled in many of the gaps in Annan's story.

History books such as Basil Davidson's *Modern Africa: A Social and Political History* (1994) provided basic information about the political and social events that influenced Annan's life. And *Basic Facts about the United Nations* (1995), a book published by the United Nations, helped me to understand the way the UN operates.

Finally, the official UN web site, *www.un.org*, provided the most current information about UN activities around the world.

FOR MORE INFORMATION

BOOKS

Bodnarchuk, Kari. *Rwanda: Country Torn Apart.* Minneapolis: Lerner Publishing Group, 1999.

Howard, Megan. *Madeleine Albright.* Minneapolis: Lerner Publishing Group, 1998.

Johnson, Edward. *United Nations—Peacekeeper?* Austin, TX: Raintree/Steck-Vaughn, 1995.

Ricciuti, Edward R. *Somalia: A Crisis of Famine and War.* Brookfield, CT: Millbrook Press, 1993.

Stefoff, Rebecca. *Saddam Hussein: Absolute Ruler of Iraq.* Brookfield, CT: Millbrook Press, 1995.

Symynkywicz, Jeffrey B. *Civil War in Yugoslavia.* Morristown, NJ: Silver Burdett Press, 1997.

Woog, Adam. *The United Nations.* San Diego: Lucent Books, 1994.

INTERNET RESOURCES

Kofi Annan, Secretary-General of the United Nations
http://www.un.org/Overview/SG/sg7bio.html
Provides a biography of Annan.

The UN Home Page
http://www.un.org
Provides a virtual guide to the United Nations and the most current information about UN activities around the world.

VISITING UN HEADQUARTERS

Tours of UN Headquarters, located at First Avenue and 46th Street in New York City, are conducted seven days a week (except Thanksgiving, Christmas, and New Year's Day) from 9:15 A.M. to 4:15 P.M. For current information about guided tours, call (212) 963-7713.

INDEX

▲ 93 ▲

ABOUT THE AUTHOR

John Tessitore is a former editor of *Maxim* magazine, a contributor to the *Christian Science Monitor,* and the author of the young adult biographies *Ernest Hemingway* and *Muhammad Ali,* published by Franklin Watts. He is currently working toward his Ph.D. in American studies at Boston University.